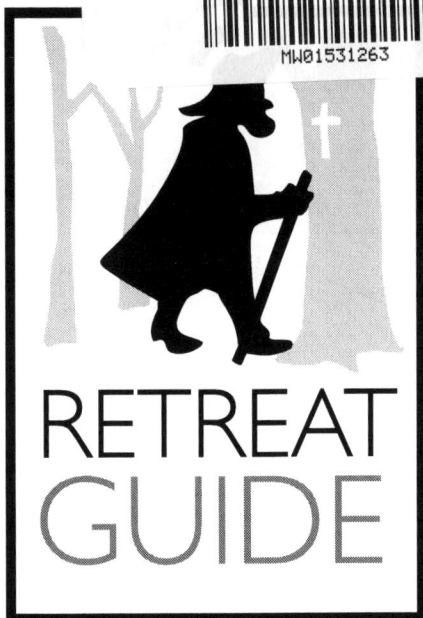

RETREAT GUIDE

A VIRGIN'S COURAGE

A RETREAT GUIDE ON ST. KATERI TEKAKWITHA

FR. JOHN BARTUNEK, LC, STHD

ISBN-10: 1548680168

ISBN-13: 978-1548680169

This booklet is a part of RCSpirituality's *Retreat Guide* service, which includes free online videos and audio tracks available at **RCSpirituality.org**.

INTRODUCTION

A Virgin's Courage

RETREAT OVERVIEW

During his last homily at his last World Youth Day, St. John Paul II spoke to almost one million young people gathered in the outskirts of Toronto, Canada about courage, about not being afraid to take a stand for Jesus Christ. In doing so, he invoked the example of the first Native American canonized saint from North America: St. Kateri Tekakwitha. He said:

...[D]o not be afraid to follow Christ on the royal road of the Cross! At difficult moments in the Church's life, the pursuit of holiness becomes even more urgent. And holiness is not a question of age; it is a matter of living in the Holy Spirit, just as Kateri Tekakwitha did here in America and so many other young people have done.

In most parts of the world, the Church is right now undergoing "difficult moments." And so, our pursuit of holiness is right now "even more urgent." This Retreat Guide on St. Kateri Tekakwitha, A Virgin's Courage, is designed to help us renew and persevere in that pursuit.

o   The First Meditation will highlight lessons from the first part of St. Kateri's remarkable life, the years in which she lived with her Mohawk tribe in what is currently Upstate New York.

o   The Second Meditation will reflect on the last three years of her life, when she lived in the St. Francis Xavier Mission village, near Montreal, Canada.

○ In the Conference we will take some time to unpack the Church's teaching regarding non-Christian religions and how we should think about them.

Let's begin by quieting our hearts and turning our attention to God, who never stops paying attention to us. Let's ask him for all the graces we need: most especially, the grace to be strengthened by the inspiring courage of the Mystic Virgin of the North American wilderness, St. Kateri Tekakwitha.

NOTES

FIRST MEDITATION

"Come, Follow Me!"

INTRODUCTION

Kateri was the daughter of a pagan Mohawk chieftain and a Christian Algonquin mother named *Lorogode* (Little Sunshine). Born in 1656, she was orphaned by the time she was four years old. The same smallpox epidemic that killed her mother and little brother, and probably her father, left young Kateri with a lifelong limp, a severely scarred and disfigured face, and permanently damaged eyesight. She habitually wore a blanket over her head as a kind of hood to shield her over sensitive eyes from light. In childhood, her handicaps were especially notable, and they are the origin of her name, "Tekakwitha," which means "she who gropes when she walks," or "she who pushes with her hands."

Kateri's uncle was a Mohawk chief just as her father had been, and he adopted her after the death of her parents, putting her under the supervision of her aunts. The orphan thus lived in their section of one of the clan's longhouses, at Caughnawa, and learned the rhythms and duties of their communal life, contributing her share of work to the upkeep of the tribe.

CLASH OF CULTURES

Catholic missionaries, mostly under the guidance of Jesuit priests, known as the Black Robes, had already been in contact with the Iroquois tribes of this area, and some ofthe Native Americans there had embraced the Catholic faith and had been baptized.

But this interaction wasn't always peaceful. Converts took up a way of life that contradicted many tribal customs, both moral and religious. They refused to practice the shamanic invocation of spirits for healing or devotion to dream prophecies. They also resisted the rampant vices of polygamy, drunkenness, and malicious gossip.

Their counter-cultural behaviors made them ready targets of blame whenever disasters or tragedies occurred. If there were an outbreak of sickness, a defeat in battle, or the death of a loved one, the Christians were blamed. They were belittled and ostracized in small ways on a daily basis, and sometimes persecuted more directly and violently.

This ongoing tension led many of the converts to move away from the tribal communities and take up residence in one of the mission centers built and governed by the French missionaries. The resulting drain on the tribal population only exacerbated the resentment of those Native Americans who didn't convert, aggravating the tensions.

KATERI'S CONTEXT

The young Kateri, who had received some instruction in the faith from her Christian mother but who had not been baptized, would have witnessed firsthand, day after day, the unfolding of this drama. Soon after her death, the tensions erupted into an all-out war that produced some of the first Native American martyrs for the faith in North America.

Kateri never learned to read or write, and since she died at such a young age, we don't know for certain how she reacted to this situation during her childhood and adolescence. But we do know that in spite of her uncle's angry resistance to the missionaries' influence in his community, and despite the suffering and even the self-imposed exile endured by the members of her tribe who converted to Christianity, God was working in her heart, drawing her towards him in hidden ways.

This was evident, first of all, through the flowering of natural virtues even before her baptism. When she finally did ask to be baptized, the missionary priest working in her village did his usual research among her companions to assure her sincerity and worthiness, and he was surprised to find that everyone spoke of her without reproach—something very unusual in that tribal culture.

GOD'S HIDDEN WORK

But the action of God's providence in her young life was most vividly present in her strong desire to stay unmarried. In the social and economic system of the Iroquois, an unmarried woman was unheard of. Yet Kateri persisted in her resolve even after extensive cajolery, ridicule, violent criticism, and trickery.This drove her uncle and aunts to distraction. But her other qualities and virtues—her patience, dependability, gentleness and industriousness—were just as persistent, so in the end they accepted her strange preference.

Later, when she eventually moved to the St. Francis Xavier Mission, she learned about the Christian vocation to consecrated virginity and rejoiced in how powerfully God had prepared and protected her to be able to desire and embrace it. Even there, however, her fellow converts were encouraging her to marry, as was the general custom. But she told them, serenely and calmly, that Jesus was and would always be her only spouse. In this way, the vague desire to belong to God alone, already present even in her adolescence, matured into a formal vow of perpetual virginity and consecration to Jesus three years after her baptism, a vow she pronounced on the Solemnity of Mary's Annunciation, March 25th, 1679.

By natural temperament Kateri was shy and soft-spoken. So throughout the years of her adolescence, even though Jesuit missionaries were present and even built a little chapel beside the longhouses of her community, she never dared to speak to one of them. Their work, and the example of others who converted and followed what the Native Americans called "the prayer", namely the Catholic faith, influenced her, but from a distance.

Her first conversation with one of the priests occurred one day when she was about 19-years-old and a bad sore on her foot forced her to stay back from working in the cornfields. She was lying on her mat in the longhouse near two elderly women who were also staying back. Jesuit priests generally didn't enter the longhouses, but that day Fr. James de Lamberville felt moved to go in to minister to the sick and the elderly. He entered the longhouse, and Kateri was overjoyed at the opportunity to converse with him. She opened her heart to him, expressing her passionate desire to receive baptism and become a follower of Jesus. She followed his indications about coming to pray and receive instruction in the chapel as soon as she had recovered, and she progressed rapidly in knowledge and piety—so much so, in fact, that the priest ended up waving the usual two-year period of catechumenate. Kateri was baptized a few months later, on Easter Sunday, 1676. She was twenty-years-old.

THE NEED FOR COURAGE

And that's when the sufferings she had seen other converts endure became her own. Besides constant ridicule and humiliating false accusations, she was also left without food or water on Sundays, because she refused to join the others working in the forests and the cornfields on the Lord's Day.

Her aunts continuously slandered and badgered her, making her an object of disdain and mockery among many of the villagers. They would even go so far as to have drunkards follow her to the chapel, shouting insults and pelting her with stones as she made her way to the tabernacle to pray.

Meanwhile, Kateri became an inspiration and a model of fidelity and piety to the other converts. But the constant persecution made a normal Christian life impossible, and following the advice of the missionary priest, she finally decided to leave her family and her community and undertake the 300-mile trek through the wilderness to the Mission of St. Francis Xavier near Montreal. She left in secret, accompanied by two missionaries and was pursued by her furious uncle, but he never caught up with her. After weeks of weary travel, she arrived safely at Sault Saint-Louis, where she was free to live without constriction as a Christian. It was five months since her baptism.

TOUGH DECISIONS

She left behind all that was familiar to her, all that she had ever known, in fact, in order to be able to live her newfound faith in freedom. And that sacrifice blossomed into meaning and joy in this life, and everlasting holiness in the next.

It must not have been easy for her to abandon the affection, approval, and customs of her tribe for a place she had never seen and a way of life she had only heard about. And yet, she found the courage to do it. Jesus meant that much to her.

Here is another lesson for us. We may wonder sometimes why we don't seem to make much progress in our pursuit of holiness and spiritual maturity. Could it be because we are reluctant to leave behind certain habits, customs, or relationships that are holding us back? Could it be that we want to receive the fruits of grace without releasing the familiar comforts of worldly mediocrity and approval, without resisting the anti-Christian cultural influences all around us?

These are worthwhile things to think about—even to pray about. And there is no better time than now to start. In the next meditation, we will look more closely at Kateri's life in the St. Francis Xavier Mission, and what it can teach us about how to grow in holiness. But for now, let's take some time to reflect prayerfully on the humble courage she displayed before she got there. The following questions and quotations may help your meditation.

QUESTIONS FOR PERSONAL REFLECTION/GROUP DISCUSSION

1. Reflecting back on my life, what are the times and ways in which God was working behind the scenes, preparing me to receive his grace? Savor and thank the Lord for this hidden work of love.

2. When have I had to face opposition or obstacles to the living out of my faith? How did I react? Speak to the Lord about these experiences, and about what he wants to teach me through them.

3. What influences or habits in my life are impeding the flow of God's grace into my heart and mind? What can I do about them?

QUOTATIONS TO HELP YOUR PRAYER

Great crowds were traveling with him, and he turned and addressed them, "If anyone comes to me without hating his father and mother, wife and children, brothers and sisters, and even his own life, he cannot be my disciple. Whoever does not carry his own cross and come after me cannot be my disciple. Which of you wishing to construct a tower does not first sit down and calculate the cost to see if there is enough for its completion? Otherwise, after laying the foundation and finding himself unable to finish the work the onlookers should laugh at him and say, 'This one began to build but did not have the resources to finish.' Or what king marching into battle would not first sit down and decide whether with ten thousand troops he can successfully oppose another king advancing upon him with twenty thousand troops? But if not, while he is still far away, he will send a delegation to ask for peace terms. In the same way, everyone of you who does not renounce all his possessions cannot be my disciple."

—Luke 14:25–33
NABRE

[But] whatever gains I had, these I have come to consider a loss because of Christ. More than that, I even consider everything as a loss because of the supreme good of knowing Christ Jesus my Lord. For his sake I have accepted the loss of all things and I consider them so much rubbish, that I may gain Christ and be found in him ... It is not that I have already taken hold of it or have already attained perfect maturity, but I continue my pursuit in hope that I may possess it, since I have indeed been taken possession of by Christ [Jesus]. Brothers, I for my part do not consider myself to have taken possession. Just one thing: forgetting what lies behind but straining forward to what lies ahead, I continue my pursuit toward the goal, the prize of God's upward calling, in Christ Jesus.

—Philippians 3:7–9, 12–14
NABRE

O God, you are my God—it is you I seek! For you my body yearns; for you my soul thirsts, In a land parched, lifeless, and without water. I look to you in the sanctuary to see your power and glory. For your love is better than life; my lips shall ever praise you! I will bless you as long as I live; I will lift up my hands, calling on your name. My soul shall be sated as with choice food, with joyous lips my mouth shall praise you! I think of you upon my bed, I remember you through the watches of the night. You indeed are my savior, and in the shadow of your wings I shout for joy. My soul clings fast to you; your right hand upholds me.

—Psalm 63:2–9
NABRE

NOTES

SECOND MEDITATION
Kateri's Secrets

INTRODUCTION

The St. Francis Xavier Mission on the banks of the St. Lawrence River was a thriving village in 1677, when Kateri Tekakwitha arrived. The French missionaries were the organizers and spiritual leaders of the community, but most of the villagers were Iroquois natives who had become Catholics and, just like Kateri, had chosen self-imposed exile from their home communities in order to be able to live their faith freely.

The Iroquois Mission included twenty-two longhouses, every longhouse being home to up to seven families, each with their own hearth inside the elongated wooden structure. A small bark-covered building served as the village chapel.

A TRULY CHRISTIAN RHYTHM

The rhythm of each day was punctuated with two Masses in the morning: one at the crack of dawn for those who wished to go to work early, and another after sunrise. During the day the villagers would engage in their subsistence work as normal: horticulture and gathering during the summer, and hunting during the winter. A bell would remind everyone to pray the Angelus during the day, and the evenings would find many of them at prayer in the chapel. Sundays were entirely dedicated to the Lord, with Masses, adoration and benediction, various times of instruction in the faith, and meetings of confraternities to pray the Rosary and attend to the sick and the dying. Here at the mission the Catholic faith was at the core not only of the converts' hearts, but also of their daily and weekly schedules.

In this atmosphere, Kateri and the other converts flourished. Three characteristics of Kateri's life stand out from this period: prayer, penance, and partnership. And we can learn something valuable from each of them.

KATERI'S PRAYER

Prayer was the beating heart of Kateri's life at Sault Saint-Louis. Everyone noticed how important prayer was to her, and how faithfully she sought the Lord in prayer. She almost always attended both of the daily Masses, and often she would rise long before dawn to go and adore the Eucharist in the tabernacle in quiet and solitude. She also loved the Rosary and kept it around her neck throughout the workday, even when she wasn't praying it.

It's remarkable to think about the intensity of her devotion to prayer and contemplation when we consider that she did not read and had no books. The presence of the Lord in the Eucharist and in her own soul, the truths of the faith as explained to her by missionaries in talks and homilies, and the Holy Spirit's gentle, enlightening guidance in the silence of her heart were enough for her.

Yet this sincere devotion to prayer never made her shirk her share of work in the community. As Fr. Pierre Cholenec—one of the priests at the mission as well as her spiritual director and first biographer—put it:

> ...[H]er devotion was all the more to be valued since it was not the idle kind in which there is usually nothing but self-love, nor was Kateri one of those

stubborn devotees who are at church when it is time to clean the house.[1]

THE WINTER HUNT

During the cold winter months, the Iroquois would leave their longhouses and go on an extended hunting excursion, since it was much easier in winter to live off the forest than to live off whatever was left from the summer gathering and planting. The men would spend the days tracking and hunting, while the women would skin and butcher the game, prepare the food, and tend to the needs of the camp. The converts who lived in the Mission continued this tradition.

Kateri accompanied one of these hunting parties during her first winter there. She sorely missed the Masses and the real presence of the Lord in the Eucharist back at the mission chapel, but even so she found ways to continue spending time alone with the Lord.

Each morning before breakfast—which was the only formal meal of the day for the Iroquois—the whole community would gather to pray. Then, before breakfast was over, Kateri would discreetly leave the camp and make her way to a little clearing in a cluster of nearby trees, which she had arranged into a living chapel by carving a cross into one of the tree trunks. In this way, at about the time when the priests were celebrating the second morning Mass at the Mission, she would be united to them through prayer. As a way of being present

---

[1] Béchard, Henri. *Kaiatanoron Kateri Tekakwitha*. Kateri Center Kahnawake, Quebec: 1994, p.95.

spiritually, she adopted the practice of asking her guardian angel to attend Mass in her place, since she couldn't be there physically.

St. Kateri made space for God in her life, no matter what, because she truly loved him and felt her need for his grace. She should inspire us to do the same.

KATERI'S PENANCES

Another striking element in Kateri's life was the importance she gave to the practice of penance and of making reparation for sins. She felt moved to voluntarily undertake sacrifices that caused her physical suffering for two reasons shared by many saints who went before her. First, she saw these penances as a way to repair for the sins of her past life and for the sins of others. Second, she saw them as a way to unite herself to the sufferings of Jesus, to accompany him and be close to him in the sorrows and pains of his Passion.

Christ's Passion spoke to Kateri in a special way, partially because in the Iroquois culture one of the primary love languages was the endurance of physical hardship. And so, Kateri's penances sometimes took dramatic form. She walked across a frozen lake with bare feet; she and a companion took turns scourging each other; she slept on thorn branches; she burned her feet with hot coals. Fr. Cholonec, had to rein in this zeal for physical penances, since some of her practices were compromising her health.

Other converts who lived in the Mission shared the tendency towards violent penitential practices, and they too had to be reined in by the Jesuit missionaries. In our own post-modern culture, where physical comfort and pleasure are afforded such high value, it may be difficult to identify with St. Kateri's desire to express her love for Christ through voluntary physical penances. And yet, maybe she has something to teach us about offering up our sufferings and discomforts. She once reflected that: "I am extremely touched by the three nails which fixed our Lord to the Cross: yet they are but an image of my sins."[2] There is profound wisdom in that simple affirmation.

KATERI'S PARTNERS IN
THE PURSUIT OF HOLINESS

Finally, it is worth noting that although Kateri abundantly nourished her spiritual life with prayer and penance, she refused to walk the path of Christian discipleship alone. Once she reached the Mission, God's providence gave her the gift of friends and companions in her adventure of faith, partners in her pursuit of holiness, and she accepted that gift.

Her closest companion was a young widow from the Oneida tribe named Mary Theresa. They and a third convert proposed starting their own order of nuns after a visit to a Montreal hospital introduced them to the consecrated life. The priests advised against it. But even so, Kateri's devotion and example attracted other spiritually sensitive women like a magnet.

Gradually and organically, they formed a natural band of devoted Christian apostles. The other members of the village referred to the group as Kateri and her sisters. They would meet regularly for prayer and also

2   Ibid., p. 109

to encourage each other in the faith—taking turns giving impromptu exhortations about love for God and neighbor. They committed themselves to a life of simplicity, joyful prayer and penance, and virtue, and they held each other accountable to those commitments. They also came up with creative ways to serve the sick and the poor, delivering bundles of wood to them under cover of night, for example, and burying the dead. This band of joyful missionary disciples continued even after Kateri's death.

KATERI'S FINAL VICTORY

Prayer, penance, and partnership—these three core elements of the Mohawk virgin's few years as a Christian enabled her spiritual life to flourish, even as her weak constitution and extraordinary penances contributed to the demise of her physical health. Off and on for the entire last year of her life, she was ill with a constant fever, stomach pains, and bouts of vomiting. In the early spring of 1680, her twenty-fourth year, she became too weak to leave her longhouse. She continued to encourage her companions through her prayers and the joyful, peaceful way she endured her suffering. Gradually the other members of the village began visiting her on her sickbed. Everyone seemed to be drawn to her, and when Fr. Cholenec granted her the privilege of receiving Holy Communion in her bed—a truly exceptional privilege in the mission village—no one was surprised or offended.

Finally, on Wednesday of Holy Week she received the anointing of the sick and at 3pm Fr Cholenec rang the village bell. All the villagers came in from their work and gathered around Kateri's mat. When the last of

Kateri's "sisters" was inside and kneeling in prayer, her agony began. She died an hour later. Her last words, whispered almost imperceptibly were, "Jesus, I love you … Jesus, Mary."

KATERI'S MIRACLES

When she breathed her last, the priest and the people remained gathered around her in prayer, commending her soul to the Lord. Fifteen minutes later her first miracle occurred. Fr. Cholenec looked up to discover that all the scarring and disfigurement she had borne ever since the smallpox epidemic when she was a little girl had completely disappeared, and her face had become marvelously, supernaturally beautiful. The missionary priest let out a loud cry and sent for his companion, who was busy preparing the altar of repose for Holy Thursday. He arrived in a rush to find the whole throng gazing in wonder at the prodigy. Later, the missionaries described the phenomenon as follows:

> Her face looked more beautiful than it had been while she was alive; it gave joy to everyone and strengthened them in the faith they had embraced; it was a new argument of credibility, which God gave [them] that they may have a taste of the faith.[3]

The next day, French visitors who had come to the village for the Holy Thursday liturgies saw Kateri on her mat and marveled at the "young woman who slept so peacefully." When they were told that she was not sleeping but dead, they rushed back into the longhouse and knelt in prayer,

3   Ibid., p. 153

not to pray to God on her behalf, but to ask for her intercession with God on their behalf. During the funeral and up until the moment of burial, the priests were unable to cover her face in the coffin, as was the usual custom, because everyone found such delight and inspiration in gazing at it.

Other miracles soon followed. Kateri appeared in visions to the missionary priests and other members of the community. Sick and dying people were cured through her intercession. Mothers in the midst of difficult deliveries would invoke her aid and name their children after her in thanksgiving for her help. Spiritual healings also occurred, especially the gift of chastity and deliverance from obsessive temptations of the flesh. As Fr. Cholenec put it, "Finally, so many healings occurred in the years that followed, that we have stopped recording them."[4]

CONCLUSION: ALL FOR US

We are not all given the joy of witnessing dramatic miracles firsthand, but every miracle belongs to all of us anyway. They are part of the story of our Catholic family, the family of those who have gone before us, sharing the same faith and the same struggles. And so we should feel free to rejoice in them.

But even more than that, we should feel encouraged and inspired when we consider the marvels God's grace worked in this unlikely candidate for sanctity. That same God, and that same grace, are still at work today in our Church and in our very own lives. If we, like Kateri, the

---

4   Ibid., p. 196

Lily of the Mohawks and the Mystic of the Wilderness, make space for Jesus in our busy lives, embrace the Cross out of love for the Lord, and welcome the gift of partners in the pursuit of holiness whenever God's providence affords them, then we, like Kateri, will discover the ever-growing joys of holiness and the meaning of everlasting love.

In the Conference, we will reflect on what the Church teaches about how we should view non-Christian religions, like the religion of the Iroquois Nation that Kateri belonged to. But for now, let's take some time to reflect prayerfully, in the silence of our hearts, on what God may be saying to us through the simple but beautiful life of St. Kateri Tekakwitha. The following questions and quotations may help your mediation.

QUESTIONS FOR PERSONAL REFLECTION/GROUP DISCUSSION

1. What do I do to carve out time for prayer in my life? Is it enough?

2. What is my attitude towards sin in general? Towards my sins? How do I tend to react to physical suffering and discomfort? How could I use those experiences to make reparation for sin?

3. Am I trying to make my journey of faith as a Lone Ranger? How much am I Investing in relationships with people who share my faith, people who through God's providence may be able to become partners in our pursuit of holiness?

Rising very early before dawn, he left and went off to a deserted place, where he prayed. Simon and those who were with him pursued him and on finding him said, "Everyone is looking for you." He told them, "Let us go on to the nearby villages that I may preach there also. For this purpose have I come." So he went into their synagogues, preaching and driving out demons throughout the whole of Galilee.

—Mark: 1:35–39

NABRE

He said to them, "Go into the whole world and proclaim the gospel to every creature. Whoever believes and is baptized will be saved; whoever does not believe will be condemned. These signs will accompany those who believe: in my name they will drive out demons, they will speak new languages. They will pick up serpents [with their hands], and if they drink any deadly thing, it will not harm them. They will lay hands on the sick, and they will recover."

—Mark 16:15–18

NABRE

The community of believers was of one heart and mind, and no one claimed that any of his possessions was his own, but they had everything in common. With great power the apostles bore witness to the resurrection of the Lord Jesus, and great favor was accorded them all. There was no needy person among them, for those who owned property or houses would sell them, bring the proceeds of the sale, and put them at the feet of the apostles, and they were distributed to each according to need.

—Acts 4:32–35

NABRE

NOTES

CONFERENCE

Are All Religions Really the Same?

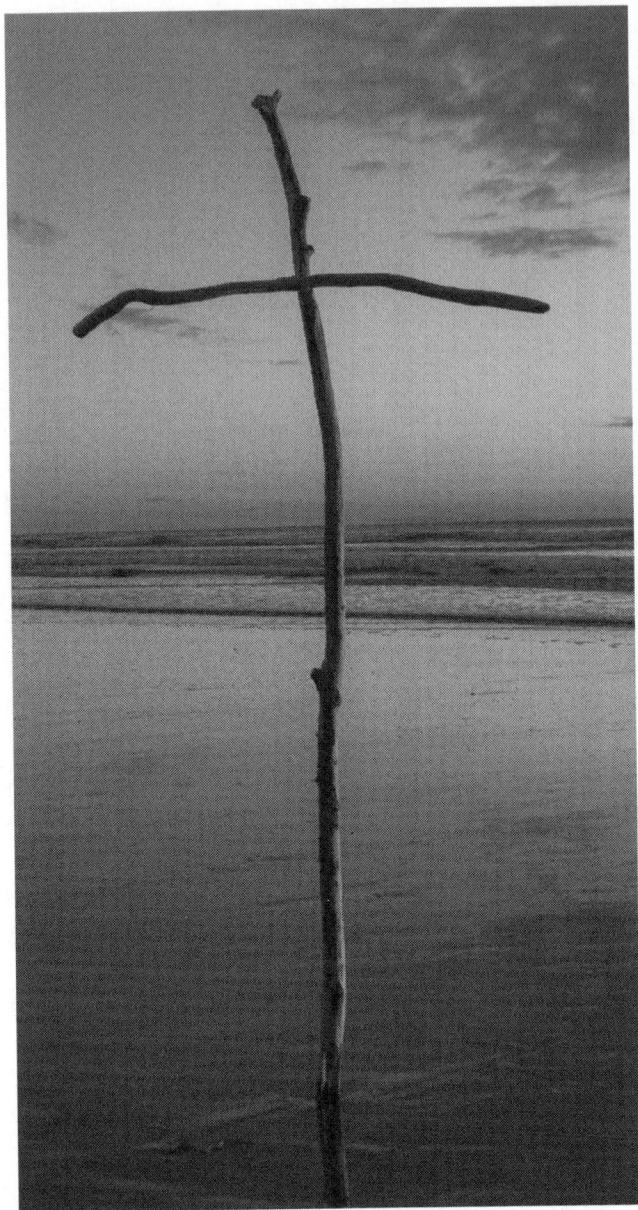

INTRODUCTION

St. Kateri Tekakwitha's path to holiness depended in large part on missionaries taking their very lives into their hands in order to bring the Good News of Jesus Christ to pagan Native Americans who had never heard that name before. Throughout the history of the Church, missionaries have been doing the same thing, seeking out people who have never heard the Gospel and courageously challenging their pagan religious traditions with the message of Christianity.

But is that still necessary today? After all, with the coming of globalization, hasn't it become clear that all religions need to be respected equally? Didn't the Second Vatican Council demand that we respect non-Christians instead of trying to convert them? And, in the end, aren't all religions basically the same anyway?

Well, as to that last question, if all religions were basically the same, then we would have to conclude that all the missionary work of the Church through the centuries has been, at the very best, a waste of time. But we know that isn't the case.

So what does the Church actually teach regarding the proper attitude towards non-Christian religions? That's what this conference will explore.

First, we will look at the context in which the Second Vatican Council made its statement about this topic—the rise of a globalized world—then we will look at the statement itself and analyze it. Finally, we will examine the practical recommendations the Church gives us for being respectful of other people without betraying the truth of Jesus Christ.

A CHANGE OF "POLICY"?

Here is how the Council's Declaration on the Relation of the Church to Non-Christian Religions, "*Nostra Aetate*" or "In Our Time" begins:

> In our time, when day by day mankind is being drawn closer together, and the ties between different peoples are becoming stronger, the Church examines more closely her relationship to non-Christian religions. In her task of promoting unity and love among men, indeed among nations, she considers above all in this declaration what men have in common and what draws them to fellowship.
>
> —*Nostra Aetate*, 1

A PRE-EMPTIVE STRIKE FOR GLOBALIZATION

As that statement shows, decades before the turn of the 21st century, the Church had already explicitly acknowledged the coming wave of globalization, in which the fate of individual nations and the fate of the whole family of nations were more closely intertwined than ever before.

In a world without telephones, Internet, airplanes, television, satellites, and nuclear weapons—and such was the world just one generation before the Council published this document, in 1965—different peoples could easily keep to themselves. Earthquakes in Iran didn't used to make headlines in Argentina. Now, however, Argentineans can watch floods in Thailand on the Internet, and email contributions to relief funds the same day.

The Church anticipated this change, and, more than any other institution, appreciated its profound cultural implications. No longer would it be rare for Catholics to come into frequent, familiar contact with non-Christians (or vice-versa); it would become an everyday occurrence—Hindus and Christians would be living in the same dorm room; Muslims would be working one office-cubicle over.

POST-MODERN DOGMAS

The challenges of a shrinking world spawned various reactions. Western culture in general began propagating the dogmas of Tolerance, Multiculturalism, and Diversity—buzzwords that have since been drained of their original meaning and power. Some specific groups, small and large, resisted the change, barricading themselves inside cultural ghettos, and at times even using extreme violence to express their disdain for the inevitable process by which "mankind is being drawn closer together."

The Church has consistently called for a different approach, one that even many Catholics have misunderstood, and consequently opposed, one based on actively engaging in the new cultural exchange, setting its agenda, and taking advantage of it.

The Council reiterated the Church's task of "promoting unity and love among men, indeed among nations." And to make this task more doable, *Nostra Aetate* set out to reflect on "what men have in common and what draws them to fellowship." It was looking for some way to build bridges between different cultures and their differing religions, instead of retreating into a fearful, self-defeating, fortress mentality.

NOT A COP-OUT

Critics of this approach accuse the Second Vatican Council of compromising the primacy of Christ, of glossing over the uniqueness and definitiveness of Christian revelation and thereby falling into religious indifferentism—a heresy claiming that all religions are basically the same.

Maybe some individual Catholics have tumbled into that error, but the Church itself hasn't. The Council's document reiterates Christ's incomparable supremacy, and the Catechism goes so far as to restate the ancient affirmation that there is no salvation outside the Church, that

> ... [A]all salvation comes from Christ the head through the Church which is his Body ... [T]o reunite all his children, scattered and led astray by sin, the Father willed to call the whole of humanity together into his Son's Church. The Church is the place where humanity must rediscover its unity and salvation
>
> —*Catechism of the Catholic Church*, 846, 845

No trace of indifferentism there.

In the same vein, the Council fathers reaffirmed the Church's task of evangelizing all cultures:

"Although in ways known to himself," they stated, "God can lead those who, through no fault of their own, are ignorant of the Gospel, to that faith without which it is impossible to please him, the Church still has the obligation and also the sacred right to evangelize all men.

—*Ad Gentes*, 7

So the Council didn't change Christian doctrine or espouse religious indifferentism, as many advocates of so-called Tolerance and Multiculturalism do. Rather, it highlighted what the different religions truly have in common, and proposed that as a starting place for building fruitful relationships, relationships that can serve to help others come to know Christ. That is, after all, the ultimate goal of all interreligious exchange; dialogue is not meant to repress evangelization. The Council even provided a prescription for the qualities of those relationships: they should be characterized by mutual understanding, respect, and common social action.

Only this approach can preserve the rich diversity of human culture in the face of globalizing forces, while at the same time opening up new avenues of exchange and cooperation, and drawing all souls closer to Christ.

Catholics can't ensure that everyone in the world will follow the Council's recommendation, but they can certainly do so themselves, and if all 1.2 billion of us did so, it would have a profound impact on the global scene. But following the Council means following a narrow path, one much more difficult than the illusory quick-fixes of Tolerance and Multiculturalism.

THE UNITY OF HUMAN NATURE

First you have to reflect deeply on what all religions have in common: human nature. The Council fathers put it beautifully when they wrote,

> One is the community of all peoples, one their origin, for God made the whole human race to live over the face of the earth. One also is their final goal, God. His providence, His manifestations of goodness, His saving design extend to all men …
>
> —*Nostra Aetate*, 1

When God looks down upon the human race, he sees his beloved children, scattered and divided by sin, some of whom have found their way back to their Father's house in the Church, but most of whom are still estranged from him, wandering in the darkness of ignorance and selfishness, like sheep who have gone far astray. But in his eyes, they are all called to be members of one family, and Christ is their Savior, their Shepherd.

This unity of human nature manifests itself in many ways, one of which is the universality of the so-called "religious sense." All people are hardwired to seek God. As the Catechism puts it,

> Man is by nature and vocation a religious being ... Man is made to live in communion with God in whom he finds happiness
>
> —*Catechism of the Catholic Church*, 44–45

Because of this, all religions, whether local tribal creeds, Hinduism, Buddhism, Islam, or Judaism, share a common endeavor—they try to satisfy this innate human longing for God.

COMMON QUESTIONS

Nostra Aetate expresses this by pointing out the basic questions that all religious doctrines try to answer, the same questions that resound in the depths of the human spirit:

> Men expect from the various religions answers to the unsolved riddles of the human condition, which today, even as in former times, deeply stir the hearts of men: What is man? What is the meaning, the aim of our life? What is moral good, what sin? Whence suffering and what purpose does it serve? Which is the road to true happiness? What are death, judgment and retribution after death? What, finally, is that ultimate inexpressible mystery which encompasses our existence: whence do we come, and where are we going?
>
> —*Nostra Aetate*, 1

These are the questions that all religions try to answer—and few questions go deeper into the human heart. And this commonality is why, at first glance, some people mistakenly think that all religions are basically the same. But although they all pose the same questions, all religions do not in any way offer the same answers. And that is why all religions are definitely not the same.

THE CHURCH'S PRESCRIPTION

Recognizing and appreciating this profound bond by which a common human nature links all individuals and all peoples is the prerequisite for following the Church's recommendation. Without assimilating that truth, striving for mutual understanding, respect, and common action between Catholics and non-Christians is a pipe-dream—with it, it's a real possibility.

If human nature is the same for all human beings, then all have the same basic rights, the same basic dignity. The promotion of that dignity and the protection of those rights provide an ample field for common action among followers of different religions. Jews and Catholics may not agree on the divinity of Christ, but they can certainly agree that we all ought to pool our resources to see that starving children get fed.

THE ROLE OF RESPECT

Similarly, true respect for other religions has to start from understanding the nature of religion, and the deep religious yearning of the human soul.

The Catechism explains that

> The Catholic Church recognizes in other religions that search, among shadows and images, for the

God who is unknown yet near since he gives life and breath to all things and wants all men to be saved. Thus, the Church considers all goodness and truth found in these religions as "a preparation for the Gospel and given by him who enlightens all men that they may at length have life."

—*Catechism of the Catholic Church*, 843

The religious yearning of the human heart is too sacred a thing to be easily dismissed or belittled—and that is why all authentic religions need to be respected.

This profound respect enables mature Catholics to honestly recognize and admit the limits and errors present in the many forms of human religious behavior. A superficial doctrine of Multiculturalism, which implicitly demeans the real differences between cultures and religions, cannot admit negative characteristics. The Catholic, on the other hand, is able to affirm with the Council Fathers,

Very often, deceived by the Evil One, men have become vain in their reasonings, and have exchanged the truth of God for a lie, and served the creature rather than the Creator. Or else, living and dying in this world without God, they are exposed to the ultimate despair.

—*Lumen Gentium*, 16

The Catholic is not afraid to try and convince the natives of Fiji that cannibalism is contrary to true religion; the dogmatic Multiculturalist wouldn't dare.

REAL UNDERSTANDING

Finally, the mutual understanding that ought to characterize relations between Catholics and non-Christians also finds its foundation in the unity of human nature. Each human heart longs for transcendence, for lasting happiness. Each religion claims to offer a different path to the fulfillment of that desire—this is the starting place for authentic dialogue. It presupposes that individuals understand thoroughly the tenets of their own faith, not only by study, but most especially by a concerted, heartfelt effort to live it out. Without understanding your own faith, you will have nothing to offer others, and you run the risk of being seduced by half-truths found in other religions. That's the first step towards mutual understanding.

The second consists in the sincere effort to understand others' beliefs, deeply, without fear, not looking just to identify the flaws and be able to point them out, but also to grasp the answers they offer to the deepest questions, the reasons behind their practices, their history.

The greatest chapters in the history of evangelization demonstrate the effectiveness of striving for mutual understanding. When saints Cyril and Methodius, for example, pioneered the faith among the Eastern Europeans, they early on decided to write an alphabet for the Slavic language, which had never before been written down. It took time and humility to learn the language and customs, but eventually they could translate the Bible into Slavic, and thus they made the revelation of Christ understandable to an entire civilization.

CONCLUSION: TOLERANCE-PLUS

The fragile dogma of Tolerance avoids this kind of deep exchange. It eschews forays into the realm of mutual understanding, because true understanding involves the frank admission of differences, which can, and often does, lead to tension, which in turn takes time and effort to overcome.

Tolerance prefers to sweep differences under the rug, to whitewash, ever so slowly, anything that reflects deep convictions; it's too big a risk to actually deal with them.

The Council Fathers saw globalization happening long before it became a buzzword. And they offered Catholics a way to approach it, a way to assure that the emerging global culture wouldn't be reduced to economic and political expediency, but would reflect the richness of the human spirit, and irrigate the seeds of truth in other religions with the fresh, bright water of Christ's Gospel.

Through respect, common social action, and mutual uderstanding, we can be effective missionaries of a globalized culture, just as the French pioneers in North America were effective missionaries of the Iroquois culture. And that is the way to raise up for the Church and the world more saints like Kateri Tekakwitha.

Take some time now to prayerfully consider the questions in the personal questionnaire, designed to help you apply these theological truths to your daily life.

PERSONAL QUESTIONNAIRE

1. How would I explain in my own words why some people tend to think that all religions are the same?

2. How would I explain in my own words why it is actually disrespectful to claim that all religions are the same?

3. How would I explain in my own words why it is important to acknowledge human nature itself as a point of unity among people of different religions?

4. Why does mutual understanding require a deep knowledge of one's own faith?

5. Why is mere tolerance a superficial solution to the problem of religious division? What important questions does it leave aside?

6. How deeply do I probe the reasons for my own faith and the faith of others? How frequently do I raise deep questions in my own reflection or in conversation with others?

7. When I am with non-Christian friends or acquaintances, how do we talk about religion? Respectfully, with openness and an interest in learning from each other? Do we fall into sterile debates—or do we whitewash our differences as if they didn't matter?

8. Would I consider myself a good representative of the Catholic faith? What might I need to change and improve to represent Christ and the Church more worthily?

9. Some of the Iroquois converted to Catholicism as a result of the French missionaries' work. But many of them didn't. How might the missionaries have reacted to that? What can I learn from that?

10. In one of his World Youth Day messages, St. John Paul II wrote: "All baptized persons are called by Christ to become his apostles in their own personal situation and in the world ... Being disciples of Christ is not a private matter. On the contrary, the gift of faith must be shared with others." What does that statement mean for me in the here-and-now of my life?

NOTES

FURTHER READING

If you feel moved to continue reflecting and praying about this theme, you may find the following books helpful:

Kaiatanoron Kateri Tekakwitha
by Henri Béchard

Saint Kateri: Lily of the Mohawks
by Matthew and Margaret Bunson

Nostra Aetate
by Second Vatican Council

The Complete Christian Collection
by Fr. John Bartunek, LC

Crossing the Threshold of Hope
by St. John Paul II

KATERI Native American Saint: The Life and Miracles of Kateri Tekakwitha
by Giovanna Paponetti

EXPLORING MORE

Please visit our website, *RCSpirituality.org* for more spiritual resources, and follow us on Facebook for regular updates: *facebook.com/RCSpirituality*

Special thanks to Debbie Graspointer for sponsoring this Retreat Guide. If you would like to support and sponsor a Retreat Guide, please consider making a donation at RCSpirituality.org.

Retreat Guides are a service of Regnum Christi and the Legionaries of Christ.
RegnumChristi.org & *LegionofChrist.org*

Produced by Coronation.
CoronationMedia.com

Developed & Self-published by RCSpirituality.
RCSpirituality.org

66095409R00033

Made in the USA
Lexington, KY
03 August 2017